EAR/CH

2/16

**Please return / renew by date shown.**
**You can renew it at:**
**norlink.norfolk.gov.uk**
**or by telephone: 0344 800 8006**
**Please have your library card & PIN ready**

**NORFOLK LIBRARY
AND INFORMATION SERVICE**

NORFOLK ITEM

30129 074 689 127

D1349211

Michael Rosen and Annemarie Young

# What is Humanism?

## How do you live without a god?

## And Other Big Questions for Kids

WAYLAND

For Emma, Elsie and Emile (M.R.)
For Anthony, Ben and Lorraine (A.Y.)

First published in 2015 by Wayland
Text copyright © 2015 Michael Rosen and
Annemarie Young

Stephen Fry's text pp14-15 © 2015 Stephen Fry;
Camila Batmanghelidjh's text pp20-21© 2015
Camila Batmanghelidjh; Philip Pullman's text
pp26-27 © 2015 Philip Pullman; Jim Al-Khalili's
text pp 30-31 © 2015 Jim Al-Khalili; Natalie
Haynes's text pp34-35 © 2015 Natalie
Haynes; Shappi Khorsandi's text pp42-43
© 2015 Shappi Khorsandi

Wayland
338 Euston Road
London NW1 3BH

Wayland Australia
Level 17/207 Kent Street
Sydney, NSW 2000

Editor: Nicola Edwards
Design: Simon Daley, Giraffe

Cover and inside artwork by Oli Frape

A catalogue record for this title is
available from the British Library.
Dewey: 211.6-dc23
ISBN  978 0 7502 8773 9
Library e-book ISBN: 978 0 7502 8774 6

Printed in China

Wayland, part of Hachette Children's Group and
published by Hodder and Stoughton Limited

www.hachette.co.uk

## THANKS

We'd like to thank:
Philip Pullman, Camila Batmanghelidjh,
Stephen Fry, Natalie Haynes, Jim Al-Khalili
and Shappi Khorsandi for sharing their
personal philosophies with us.
Julia Adams and Jeff Round for sharing
their celebrations.
The British Humanist Association for their
support, and the American Humanist
Association for the Ten Commitments.
Dr Brian Rosen, Scientific Associate, Natural
History Museum, for his invaluable help with
the science pages.
Professor Jane Heal, University of Cambridge
and Fellow of the British Academy, for her
positive comments on the text and especially
on the morality pages.
Marianne Talbot, who was Chair of the National
Forum for Values in Education and the Community,
for her help with the Statement of Values.

## ACKNOWLEDGEMENTS

The authors and publisher would like to thank
the following for allowing these pictures to
be reproduced: Back cover (left) Courtesy of
Goldsmiths, University of London, (right) Anthony
Robinson; p4 Shutterstock.com; p5 (top to
bottom) Claire Newman Williams; Alan Moyle;
KT Bruce, Dan Mersh, University of Surrey,
Kids Company; p7 Wikimedia Commons;
p8 Courtesy of Goldsmiths, University of London;
p10 Anthony Robinson; p12 Wikimedia Commons;
p14 Claire Newman Williams; p16 Featureflash/
Shutterstock.com; p20 Kids Company;
p25 Shutterstock.com; p26 KT Bruce; p29
Wikimedia Commons; p30 University of Surrey;
p32 Wikimedia Commons; p33 Wikimedia
Commons; p34 Dan Mersh; pp36-39 Curtis
Round (www.curtisround.com); p40 Illustration
© 2004 Quentin Blake from MICHAEL ROSEN's
SAD BOOK written by Michael Rosen, illustrated
by Quentin Blake. Reproduced by permission
of Walker Books Ltd, London SE11 5HJ.
www.walker.co.uk; p42 Alan Moyle.

# Contents

# Introducing humanism

This book is not going to tell you what to think, or try to persuade you to become a humanist. Our aim is to get you to think for yourself about the big questions, such as 'Where do moral values come from?', 'Does it matter whether or not god exists?', 'Why am I here?', and see how these questions affect your life.

## Why do we need this book?

There are many books about the main religions of the world, but not many that explain non-religious worldviews such as humanism. Many people don't follow a religion or believe in a god, but still lead ethical and meaningful lives. These people use reason, science and compassion to live fulfilling, moral lives. They might not call themselves humanists, but they follow humanist principles. We want more people to understand what these principles are.

We think it's important that everyone, whether they are religious or non-believers, should think about the big questions and should never just accept what they are told. This doesn't mean you can't continue to have religious belief, but if you do you will know that it's your own, not just an unthinking acceptance of someone else's ideas.

"I have a problem with religion or anything that says, 'We have all the answers,' because there's no such thing as 'the answers'. We're complex. We change our minds on issues all the time. Religion leaves no room for human complexity."

DANIEL RADCLIFFE
ACTOR

# How the book works

We'll give you an introduction to what humanism is all about, then tell you our own reasons for being humanists. After that we'll tackle these and other questions: What is humanism? What do humanists believe? Can you be good without god or religion? Where do moral values come from? How did the earth begin? What's the purpose of life? And we'll give you an overview of humanist ideas through history.

We'll explain how humanists mark events like marriage and death, and show you what humanist weddings, funerals and naming ceremonies are like.

Philip Pullman, Camila Batmanghelidjh, Jim Al-Khalili, Natalie Haynes, Shappi Khorsandi and Stephen Fry have written about their own personal philosophies, and these are spread through book.

You will also find quotes from other people, and questions for you to think about as you read. And at the end you'll have the chance to write your own personal philosophy, using the 'think about' questions as a starting point.

STEPHEN FRY

SHAPPI KHORSANDI

PHILIP PULLMAN

NATALIE HAYNES

JIM AL-KHALILI

CAMILA BATMANGHELIDJH

## Think about

Do you believe in a god?

If yes, what does that belief mean to you?

If you don't believe in a god, why not?

# What is a humanist?

Humanists think that the answers to questions such as 'What is the purpose of life?' or 'How did we get here?' do not come from what people say are a god's opinions or thoughts. We think that they can only come from human thought and what human beings have investigated or figured out. Or, put another way, the answers to these questions can only include what is in our minds and what is in the universe. As we discover more and more about our minds and about the universe, so will we get more of an idea about the origins of life.

## Words humanists use

An **atheist** is someone who does not believe in any kind of god. Humanists are atheists but emphasise that they believe in human thought and action. Some atheists do not say they are humanists because they don't want to give the impression that they believe all human beings are equally good.

An **agnostic** is a person who thinks that the existence of a greater power, such as a god, cannot be proven or disproved. So agnostics will not say for certain that a god does or does not exist.

**Secularism** is a description of how national institutions such as governments, law courts, hospitals, schools and national ceremonies can be run, without reference to any religion or god. Most humanists think that this is the best, and most peaceful, way for things to be run so that people of one faith don't end up ruling over people of another faith, or over those who have no religious belief.

- We think that anyone can live a good life: both people who are religious and those who have no religious beliefs.
- We believe that we have only one life, and that we should do the best we can throughout the time we are alive.
- We think that we can enjoy and benefit from the very best things that other human beings have invented, thought about and made.
- We think that there are many enjoyable and useful ways to improve the world: sometimes this needs careful, logical thought – also called reason; sometimes it needs 'hunches' – usually called intuition; sometimes it needs our feelings for others – also called empathy.
- We believe that our actions should be supported by evidence, collected by people who research nature and human behaviour.
- We think that it's not enough to try to be a happy individual; we should also try to think of ways in which others – perhaps, everyone – can be happy.
- Most humanists think that it is wrong to take another person's life, whether that is by murder or execution, and some humanists oppose all wars.

**Think about**

Do you think we should be tolerant of other people's beliefs?
If you do, why is it important?
If you don't, why not?
Either way, how does this affect how you behave?

Most humanists think that government, law courts, schools and national ceremonies should be secular, with no religion involved. At the same time, most humanists think that there should be religious toleration. That is, that people should be free to practise their religion so long as it doesn't persecute or harm others.

**"An atheist believes that a hospital should be built instead of a church ⋯ that deed must be done instead of prayer said. An atheist strives for involvement in life and not escape into death. An atheist wants disease conquered, poverty vanished, war eliminated."**

MADALYN MURRAY O'HAIR (1919-1955)
AMERICAN WRITER AND ACTIVIST

# MY HUMANISM

## Michael Rosen

Michael Rosen is Jewish in origin. He's a writer for adults and children, a broadcaster and Professor of Children's Literature at Goldsmiths, University of London.

## My personal philosophy

Everyone has a 'personal philosophy'. It's made up of your thoughts about things like 'What is right?', 'What is wrong?' and 'What is the best way to live your life, or the best way for people to treat each other?'.

It can also be about thoughts like 'What is beautiful?', 'What is funny?', 'What is sad?'. Or 'Why do human beings exist?', 'Are human beings alone in the universe or is there a god or some gods who know what we are doing?', 'What happens when we die?'.

I start from the idea that everything we human beings do and think comes from us; there isn't anything apart from human beings, no god or gods to organise or run things for us.

### Think about

What are the things that are important to you?

Do you think you should behave as if you have only one life?

So all those questions about right and wrong and the rest are all things that I have to figure out through listening, reading and talking with other people.

## Then what?

Most of us try to do things that are good for ourselves and our loved ones. I do this but then I see that millions of people who try to do things that are good for themselves and their loved ones also struggle to earn enough, to stay well enough to look after their children and grandparents. So perhaps it's not enough to do things that are just good for us and our loved ones. I can see that when we look at all the things that humans make (thanks to the minds and muscles of all the human beings), some people get much more out of it than others. What comes out of all that work is not fairly shared out. I think this is wrong.

So, this leads me to think, what can we do to make it fair? It's pointless to think I can do this on my own. I'd just end up being a big boss ordering people about. I think we have to try to work with people in ways that are fair for all — never thinking that this or that person is worse or better than me because of what they look like or because of where they were born.

## My favourite quote

My favourite quote is from the play *Hamlet* by Shakespeare. Hamlet is wondering what to do, so he asks if it's worth existing ('to be or not to be') and then wonders if it's worth fighting against the difficult things ('the sea of troubles'), and if you do ('by opposing them') will that 'end them'?

*"To be, or not to be, that is the question —*
*Whether 'tis nobler in the mind to suffer*
*The slings and arrows of outrageous fortune,*
*Or to take arms against a sea of troubles,*
*And by opposing, end them?"*

This is one of the great questions facing humanists because we don't appeal to a supernatural being, or a priest, to help us answer it. We do it through thinking, reading, listening, talking, writing and experimenting with the things around us, and through working with others.

# Annemarie young

Annemarie Young's parents were born and grew up in Egypt; her maternal grandfather was from Acre, Palestine, and her other grandparents came from Russia, Scotland and Italy. She was a publisher, and now writes stories and information books for children.

## Why am I a humanist?

For me, being a humanist is liberating and life affirming. Instead of spending precious time wondering about the existence of a god or an afterlife, or being 'good' because of a fear of punishment after death, I can concentrate on living a good life in the here and now. I can try to do good for myself and those around me, and also do what I can to help make the world a fairer and better place for everyone.

## I was once religious

Even though my father was an atheist and my mother a believer in a spiritual life rather than a religious one, I was sent to a Catholic school because my parents thought I would get a good education there. So, from an early age I was imbued with religious ideas at school, and I have a vivid memory of crying because, aged six, I believed that my parents would go to hell because they did not go to church on Sundays. I'd been told that missing mass on

Sundays was a 'mortal sin', in the same category as murder, and the punishment was hell. My wonderful mother tried her best to console me, saying "Are we bad people? Do we do terrible things?" "No!" I would cry, and her response was "Then we won't go to hell. What matters is how we live our lives, not petty rules."

**Think about**

Do you think there is an afterlife, or a day of judgement after you die, when it's decided whether you go to heaven or hell? If you do, how does that affect the way you behave? If not, how does that affect your behaviour?

## What drives me now?

I followed those rules for a while, and held all the beliefs, until I was 16, when I started to question them. One day we had a discussion in class about the church's stand on contraception and on the war in Vietnam. Our excellent teacher, a nun, was not dogmatic, instead she argued from a strong ethical standpoint, and I began to wonder why we clung to the authority of god and the church. Wouldn't it be better to think about the ethics and morality of our actions from the point of our humanity? My 'faith' dissolved and I felt free to think for myself. I realised I had choices, and I must also take responsibility for my choices.

For me the most important questions are not 'How did we get here?' or 'Does god exist?'. I'm much more interested in how we, humanity, can increase the amount of good and minimise the harm we do, to each other and to the planet. And in how I can live an interesting, enjoyable and meaningful life.

## My favourite quotes

This is a quote from one of my favourite authors, George Eliot. She's telling us that we must act for ourselves and not wait for things to happen:

*"It will never rain roses: when we want to have more roses we must plant more trees."*

Edward Said, another favourite author, said:

*"Humanism is the only ... resistance we have against the inhuman practices and injustices that disfigure human history."*

11

# What is the purpose of life?

Some people seem to be able to live their lives without wondering about this. This means that their purpose in life is explained or expressed through what they do.

Some people try to get on with their lives but also wonder what it's all for. The tough message from humanists is that there is no purpose for life other than whatever you or I or she or he comes up with! We have no god or god's message or god's words to go to in order to find out and we don't go to priests or rabbis or imams in order to figure out what god's words might be. We say that it's down to us to figure it out. We might read or listen to other people, or we might just sit and think about it on our own.

"With these brains, we have the ability to question; if we fail to do that, if we look for a high priest or elder to do our thinking for us, to instruct us and manipulate us, then we are failing to live up to our potential."

ROBIN INCE
COMEDIAN, ACTOR AND WRITER

# This means that one purpose of life for humanists is to figure out the purpose of life!

Most humanists believe that no human being is less or more worthy of life than any other. Now, flowing from that, different humanists believe in different things. Some might say, for example, that the fact that we are all human doesn't mean that as we go through life we are really equal, nor should we try to be. What we should be is 'good' or as good as we possibly can be. That would be a purpose of life. Others say that the fact that we are all human means that we are all 'brothers and sisters' and that we should try to be as equal as possible. This means doing all we can to bring this about. This too would be a purpose of life.

**Think about**
What do you think is the purpose of life?

## One life

Humanists believe that we humans have one life: we are born, we change from being children to being adults; all through our lives we have relationships, some close, some not so close, some loving, some not so loving, some, perhaps, full of other emotions. Some humans make babies, some don't, and we all die. These different stages are sometimes thought of as 'rites of passage' and many humanists like to mark these moments with ceremonies. These too are about the purpose of life because they celebrate important stages in our lives and celebrate that person or people, saying to everyone there that we love them.

For some humanists, then, the purpose of life is to love each other.

# MY HUMANISM

Stephen Fry is a writer, a stage and screen actor, a comedian, a television presenter, and a campaigner on mental health issues. We asked him about what being a humanist means to him.

## What is a humanist?

A humanist is someone who will never tell you what to believe. We will never tell you what is absolutely true. We will never make claims that cannot be proven and that you cannot find out for yourself.

We believe life is an adventure and that nobody knows the answers or the destination. Anybody who tells you they know for sure what happens to us after we die is surely either a liar or a fool? For no one has ever returned from death (except in story books) to tell us.

## Doesn't it upset you to think that this life is all there is?

Some people think that believing this life is all there is makes for a rather upsetting view of our existence. If you stop and think for a while, the opposite is true. I throw everything I have into living as much as I possibly can, for if this is the only life we have it makes sense to try as much as possible to live life to the absolute full,

14

without trusting that some divine being will grant one (on the basis of no evidence) an eternity in paradise, whatever that means. I cannot think of anything duller. To live forever without my body… eugh!

## What do you think of the idea of there being a god who is looking after us?

If there is a god, he or she must be very cruel and — I think the right word is *capricious* — acting by whim and fancy rather than by consistent morals. Bone cancer in children? Earthquakes and natural disasters that kill millions of innocent people? Mosquitos? Surely a kind, loving god would never have visited such horror and misery on so many. I know much of the world's ills are our fault, but most of them are part of the pattern of nature. Over a hundred years ago Darwin showed how life developed through evolution and the ruthless survival of the fittest. Almost all animals in the wild live lives of hunger, stress, fear and danger in order to survive and pass on their genes. That's how nature works.

> 66 Darwin never had genetics to prove his case, just good science and observation. But since his day there can be surely no doubt that we are the result not of biblical creation but the beautiful unwinding of nature. Genes show that he was right. 99

## How can you have morality without religion?

You don't have to believe in a creator to know right from wrong: in fact the history of the world shows us that the less people believed in a mighty god, the kinder and more progressive in their attitudes towards slavery, minorities and plain decency they became. Voting for all, equal rights for all — these are all things constantly challenged more by the religious than by humanists.

Humanists do not claim to know, we just ask you to be very wary of those who do claim to know. Who told them? What does their knowledge mean? Why should you trust them?

Above all, don't take my word for it either. Don't take *anybody's* word for it. Find out for yourselves. Happy living!

# Can you be good without gods or religion?

## Where do moral values come from?

Humanists believe that morality – being good or at least doing no harm – is based on human nature and human experience. We base our morality on guiding principles rather than inflexible rules that can't be challenged because a religious authority says they have been handed down from a supernatural being.

The welfare and happiness of humanity is at the centre of humanist morality and ethics.

We humans have evolved as a social species and we need to cooperate with each other. Empathy, compassion and reason are essential elements in the development of human society, and these form the basis of humanist morality. Selfishness, aggression and other such characteristics are also aspects of human nature and this is why human societies develop moral values, to balance and counteract those incompatible elements.

> "Humanism is important because having a non-supernatural worldview allows you to make more ethical choices based on a general desire to do the most possible good."
>
> TIM MINCHIN
> COMEDIAN, ACTOR
> AND MUSICIAN

## The Golden Rule

Humanists don't have a simple set of rules, but there is a basic principle which underlies our morality. It is known as the 'Golden Rule', and seems to be universal to all the traditions – religious and philosophical. The Golden Rule can be stated positively as: 'Treat other

## Some examples of the Golden Rule from around the world

I will act towards others exactly as I would act towards myself.
*From a Buddhist text, about 500 BCE*

This is the sum of duty: Do nothing to others Which, if done to you, could cause you pain.
*Hindu text, about 150 BCE*

Love your neighbour as yourself.
*Judaism and Christianity, from the Torah and the Bible, about 400 BCE and again 1st Century Common Era*

None of you truly believes, until you wish for your brothers and sisters what you wish for yourself.
*Islam – from a saying of The Prophet Muhammad, 7th Century CE*

**Think about**
What do you think about the Golden Rule? Would the world be a better place if everyone acted in this way?

people in a way you would like to be treated yourself'. But the negative version: 'Do not treat others as you would not like to be treated yourself', is easier to follow. It is not difficult to understand what would cause another person harm or suffering, and to recognise that we should consider the personal interests of others before acting.

Humanists make the Golden Rule the foundation for other principles. Care for others, for example, since we would want people to be kind to us should we need it. On the other hand, it is clear that violence and killing, stealing, bullying and dishonesty are all unacceptable under this rule.

'Do not treat others as you would not like to be treated yourself' is a very general principle, and it requires empathy and understanding of others, which is something that develops as we grow up. And it also requires thought, as do all moral principles, even for people who follow the rules set down by different religions. For example, are there any circumstances when lying, or even stealing, can be justified?

# Values and laws

## Shared values

The Universal Declaration of Human Rights, which was adopted by the United Nations General Assembly in 1948, after the Second World War, is underpinned by the belief that all human beings share the same basic needs and values and that we are all entitled to these rights. This doesn't mean that there are never arguments about these rights and how they should be interpreted, but the Declaration sets out the fundamental principles.

## The Ten Commitments

Across the world, people are in broad agreement about moral values. These ten guiding principles are put forward by the American Humanist Association for teaching moral values in schools.

1   Altruism
2   Caring for the World Around Us
3   Critical Thinking
4   Empathy
5   Ethical Development
6   Global Awareness
7   Human Rights
8   Peace and Social Justice
9   Responsibility
10  Service and Participation

"I'd like my three-year-old daughter Lily to grow up to be free to make her own decisions about what she believes. To doubt, to question, to make mistakes and learn from them, to love whoever she wants and be kind to everyone, whatever their background. More than anything, I'd like her to be happy, and to endeavour to make others happy too."

ARIANE SHERINE
COMEDY WRITER, JOURNALIST
AND CAMPAIGNER

## Interpreting values

How we – people in general – interpret particular moral questions varies. For example, everyone agrees that murder is wrong, but we might disagree on what counts as murder, or on whether or when it is justifiable to go to war. Most people who live in our society share the same broad values that are the basis of our laws, but we can also work to change laws that we believe are unfair or unjust.

While we share many values with others in our society, there are some we don't share. People have different beliefs about religion, for instance, and there are specific values and rules associated with certain religions, for example about diet or dress.

You can see that deciding on your own rules is not completely straightforward. Killing someone, whether deliberately or by accident is much more serious than telling a 'white lie' to protect someone's feelings. We are fortunate to live in a society which has a sound basis of laws and ways of deciding on and changing laws. The first act, killing, is forbidden by law, whereas the second is a personal choice.

**Think about**
How do you decide for yourself whether to lie or not – especially if no one else is going to find out?

# Camila Batmanghelidjh

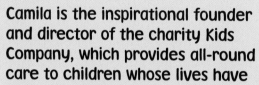

Camila is the inspirational founder and director of the charity Kids Company, which provides all-round care to children whose lives have been disrupted by poverty, abuse and trauma. Camila has won many awards and honours, including Honorary Doctorates from several universities and a CBE for services to children and young people. We asked Camila about what living a good life means to her.

## How do you get to be good and why should you?

When you play in a sandpit the sand takes on the shape of whatever you do. If you press your hands into it, the sand takes the shape of your hand and it will be reflected back at you. Being good is very similar. If you are kind and help people, then life takes that print and reflects it back, so people will be kind and want to help you.

In showing tenderness towards others, you not only experience the best of yourself but other people want to do the best for you.

When people exchange goodness between each other, they become very energetic and happy. It's a sort of unspoken law. So I reckon it's worth being good just for the energy and happiness it creates for everyone involved. But the deal is that you have to be genuine about your kindness without expecting anything back. You cannot use kindness as a tricky exchange.

## Do you have to believe in god or a religion to be able to be good?

No, you don't. Some people find it helpful to be guided by a religion, and have stories about prophets or gods to help them direct their good intentions. It's okay if you find that way of thinking helpful, but you can also be good by sticking to common sense. The most important thing is to think about what sort of person you want to be. Make your personal rules and then try to stick to them. So you can make rules not to hurt people and,

> **In showing tenderness towards others, you not only experience the best of yourself but other people want to do the best for you.**

if you break that rule, then you need to repair it with the person you've hurt by apologising to them. Just having rules promoting kindness, generosity, empathy, honesty and fun without harming anyone makes for a pretty wonderful personalised belief system. Religion is one way of believing, but you can choose different ways of believing and, as long as they bring happiness to you and other people, it's okay.

## What is hell or heaven?

Some religions believe that these are places that bad and good people go to after they die. But you could have little heavens and little hells that are with us in our life now. Some of them are created by other people's cruelty, some of them by our own cruelty, and some are random misfortunes of nature. Where we can control things to make them better, we should. Where we can't, we have to develop a non-blaming acceptance: no point in fussing over something you can't control.

Creating your own good rules to live by is like making a delicious cake and getting to eat it.

# A statement of values

A few years ago, the government set up a forum, a large group of people from all over England and Wales, to draw up a 'statement of values in education and the community'. The forum was asked to decide whether there are any values that are commonly agreed on across society. It produced a secular statement, with no reference to any religion.

## The self

We value ourselves as unique human beings capable of spiritual, moral, intellectual and physical growth and development.

On the basis of these values, we should:

* develop an understanding of our own characters, strengths and weaknesses

* develop self-respect and self-discipline

* clarify the meaning and purpose in our lives and decide, on the basis of this, how we believe that our lives should be lived

* make responsible use of our talents, rights and opportunities

* strive, throughout life, for knowledge, wisdom and understanding

* take responsibility, within our capabilities, for our own lives.

The statement was divided into four sections: The self, Relationships, Society and The environment, and you can read them on the following pages. While the statement doesn't include all possible moral values and choices, it does provide a sound and useful basis for making moral decisions.

This text was sent out to several thousand schools, national organisations and individuals, and they were asked whether they agreed with it. About 90% agreed, which shows that despite the many differences between people, there are values that the great majority share.

**Think about**

What do you think about these values?

Which values are most important for you?

## Relationships

We value others for themselves, not only for what they have or what they can do for us. We value relationships as fundamental to the development and fulfilment of ourselves and others, and to the good of the community.

On the basis of these values, we should:

* respect others, including children
* care for others and exercise goodwill in our dealings with them
* show others they are valued
* earn loyalty, trust and confidence
* work cooperatively with others
* respect the privacy and property of others
* resolve disputes peacefully.

# Society

We value truth, freedom, justice, human rights, the rule of law and collective effort for the common good. In particular, we value families as sources of love and support for all their members, and as the basis of a society in which people care for others.

On the basis of these values, we should:

- ✳ understand and carry out our responsibilities as citizens
- ✳ refuse to support values or actions that may be harmful to individuals or communities
- ✳ support families in raising children and caring for dependants
- ✳ support the institution of marriage
- ✳ recognise that the love and commitment required for a secure and happy childhood can also be found in families of different kinds
- ✳ help people to know about the law and legal processes
- ✳ respect the rule of law and encourage others to do so
- ✳ respect religious and cultural diversity
- ✳ promote opportunities for all
- ✳ support those who cannot, by themselves, sustain a dignified lifestyle
- ✳ promote participation in the democratic process by all sectors of the community
- ✳ contribute to, as well as benefit fairly from, economic and cultural resources
- ✳ make truth, integrity, honesty and goodwill priorities in public and private life.

# The environment

We value the environment, both natural and shaped by humanity, as the basis of life and a source of wonder and inspiration.

On the basis of these values, we should:

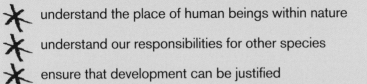

- accept our responsibility to maintain a sustainable environment for future generations
- understand the place of human beings within nature
- understand our responsibilities for other species
- ensure that development can be justified
- preserve balance and diversity in nature wherever possible
- preserve areas of beauty and interest for future generations
- repair, wherever possible, habitats damaged by human development and other means.

"The mystery of the beginning of all things is insoluble by us; and I for one must be content to remain an Agnostic."

CHARLES DARWIN
(1809-1882)
NATURALIST AND
GEOLOGIST AND
AUTHOR OF *ON THE
ORIGIN OF SPECIES*

## MY HUMANISM

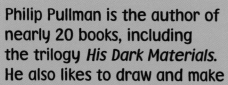
Philip Pullman

Philip Pullman is the author of
nearly 20 books, including
the trilogy *His Dark Materials*.
He also likes to draw and make
things out of wood. His books have won many awards and
prizes, among them the Carnegie of Carnegies for *Northern
Lights* and the Whitbread Book of the Year Award, and
several of them have been adapted for film and television.
Philip was presented with the Eleanor Farjeon Award for
children's literature in 2002. We asked him about the
universe and the role human beings play within it.

### What is the biggest mystery of the universe?

I believe that the universe is immense. The more we discover, the
bigger it seems to be. And the thing that makes it possible to think
and discover, our brain, is so complex that we've only begun to
explore how it works.

The biggest mystery, it seems to me, is consciousness. If we're
made of matter, as we seem to be, and if we're conscious, as we
are, then clearly matter is capable of being conscious. Given that,
it seems silly to say that only human beings can be conscious.
Animals? Plants? Stones? The air? Dark matter? Why not?

## How can we best judge what is useful and good?

Religion claims two things, basically. The first is 'This is how things began'. The second is 'This is what you must do'.

The first claim makes no sense, because in the first place each religion says something different, and in the second place science gives a much more convincing account of the origin of the universe than any religion does.

The second claim is much more important. Some religions say things like 'You must love one another, you must look after the poor and the sick, you must be truthful and kind in all your dealings'. It's hard to find any fault with that. Others seem to say things like 'You must kill everyone who doesn't agree with what this religion says'.

> 66 The only way we can judge what's useful and good, and what's crazy and cruel, is by stepping outside religion altogether, and just judging by human standards: which is a better way to live? Can we take what's useful and good, and leave what's crazy and cruel? 99

It's easy to see what's wrong with that. The trouble is that some religions say both kinds of thing. The only way we can judge what's useful and good, and what's crazy and cruel, is by stepping outside religion altogether, and just judging by human standards: which is a better way to live? Can we take what's useful and good, and leave what's crazy and cruel?

## Does it matter what people believe?

When I'm writing a story, I believe in all kinds of things: ghosts, gods and devils, magic, superstition. I believe contradictory things. I don't want certainty, I want possibility. I find that a useful and productive and enjoyable state of mind.

I don't mind if someone believes that the universe was created in six days: what matters is not what they believe but what they do. Are they kind? Are they honest? That matters much more than what goes on inside their heads. If they believe something that seems strange to me, I don't want to condemn them: I'm fascinated to hear what it's like to believe that. The universe is very big.

# Life - how did it all begin?

Humanists believe that the way to find out such things is to be like detectives: considering the evidence by looking, listening and measuring; then coming up with 'conclusions' which explain what we've found. If we find something new that doesn't fit those conclusions then we have to change what we think.

## The Big Bang

In 1929, the astronomer Edwin Hubble discovered that the universe is expanding. All the stars and galaxies are moving away from each other. So, many scientists now agree that the universe started from some kind of tiny fireball which exploded about 14,000 million years ago. This is called the 'Big Bang'. What caused the Big Bang? Scientists say we don't know yet and until we have some evidence, it's OK to stick with 'we don't know'. People also often ask what was there before the Big Bang but for scientists this is a non-question, for now. Time as we know it didn't exist in the first moments, the standard laws of physics did not apply, and there is no evidence. So we have to wait for further research.

One tiny part of the universe where we live is what we call 'Earth'. Millions of years after the Big Bang, our Milky Way galaxy formed, and eventually, about 4,600 million years ago, our Solar System, including the Sun and Earth, was born. As Earth cooled down, it formed layers, some molten (like the outer core), and some solid (like the outermost 'crust'). Heat flows upwards in streams from deep in the Earth. When these streams of heat reach the deeper crust, patches of crust sometimes melt and if this comes to the surface, we see it as lava when volcanoes erupt.

By about 3,800 million years ago, the Earth had its crust, it had seas but the air or 'atmosphere' was full of carbon dioxide and other gases, and not much oxygen.

From about 3,500 million years ago we find the earliest fossil evidence of life. These are single cells, held together in long lines,

## Think about

What do you think about the origins of life and what the scientists say?

How does that compare with what the major religions say?

What do you think?

> "I do not believe in a personal God ... If something is in me which can be called religious then it is the unbounded admiration for the structure of the world so far as our science can reveal it."

ALBERT EINSTEIN (1879-1955)
THEORETICAL PHYSICIST AND PHILOSOPHER OF SCIENCE WHO DEVELOPED THE GENERAL THEORY OF RELATIVITY

like beads on a string. Other kinds of evidence, however, suggest that life started as separate bacteria-like cells at least 500 million years earlier than that.

## Primeval soup

In 1871, Charles Darwin wondered if life started in a 'warm little pond' rich in the ingredients of which life is made. Early in the 20th century another scientist, Alexander Oparin, coined the term 'primeval soup' – primeval meaning from the beginning of time. In the Earth's crust and atmosphere there existed all that you find in living creatures. What was needed for life were the right conditions – not too hot or too cold, not too bright, not too dark, enough amounts of the right gases – and something for living things to feed off.

By around 3,000 million years ago, some new kinds of early organisms appeared that pumped out oxygen, and this changed our atmosphere forever.

From 1,500 million years ago, some organisms started to become more 'complex'. People who study fossils find evidence from around 800 million years ago of living things that look like jellyfish and sponges. Then about 540 million years ago, there was a huge increase in the numbers of worm-like animals and creatures with hard outsides.

## Evolution

In the late 18th and early 19th centuries, a number of scientists who studied living animals, plants and fossils, thought that the evidence suggested these things came about through evolution. Later, in the mid-19th century, Charles Darwin and Alfred Russel Wallace proposed the theory of evolution by natural selection, for all plants and animals, including we humans. Most humanists accept this too.

# MY HUMANISM

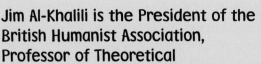

## Jim Al-Khalili

Jim Al-Khalili is the President of the British Humanist Association, Professor of Theoretical Physics at the University of Surrey and a Fellow of the Royal Society. He says: "I am a physicist, author and broadcaster. I also happen to be, like most people I know, a humanist and an atheist. But those terms don't define me. First and foremost I am a scientist." We asked him about science, humanism and religion.

## When you learn about the wonders of the universe, its structure and complexity, why doesn't that convince you that it could not have come about by accident and that there must have been a Creator?

Learning about the nature of space and time or the structure of atoms fills me with awe and wonder; it makes me want to learn more. I see a beauty in the laws of nature that can be explained by science. For me, to simply say 'it is so wonderful, it must have been designed by a Creator' is to avoid the issue. After all, who then designed the Creator?

## If something in your life, nature or the universe can't be explained, does that bother you?

Yes it does. A lot. That's why I love science. It gives me tools to find those answers. Just stating that things are the way they are because God made them that way doesn't satisfy me. I want the deeper truth.

## As president of the British Humanist Association, do you think it's important that people know about humanism?

Yes, I do. I didn't know about it until relatively recently. Then I discovered that it is in fact exactly how I want to live my own life and view the world. Humanism to me is about believing in humankind's ability to be good, compassionate and kind. Not because they are told to by a holy book or because they are afraid they will be punished in hell, but simply because they want to.

## Do you think schools should teach religion?

Yes, of course they should. The great world religions have shaped the modern world, society and culture. We cannot ignore that. But we need to understand all belief systems. Not only are they part of our shared history and heritage, they have also taught us important lessons. But so have other, non-religious, ideas. And like religions, some of these have been good for humanity, like humanism and enlightenment, and some have been evil, like Fascism. All these ideas have to be taught at school. But what I disagree with is forcing school children to believe in one view over all others, such as is done in faith schools.

> 66 Just stating that things are the way they are because God made them that way doesn't satisfy me. I want the deeper truth. 99

The idea that everything we do and think is decided by human beings alone, without a god or gods to guide us, has been around for a long time.

## India and China

One of the first atheist philosophers we know of came from India. He was called Ajita Kesakambali, and he lived about 2,500 years ago. The philosophy was called Cārvāka, later known as Lokâyata. The Cārvāka idea is that we are made up of four elements, earth, water, fire and air and that the only things that exist are what we can perceive – what we can see, hear, taste, feel or smell, and that there is no world other than here, no heaven and no hell.

Around the same time, an Ancient Chinese thinker called Fan Zhen said that he believed that there is no life after death, no everlasting soul, just as there is no sharpness of a knife left over after the knife has been destroyed.

## Charles Bradlaugh

Charles Bradlaugh (1833 –1891) was a political activist and one of the most famous English atheists of the 19th century. He founded the National Secular Society in 1866, and was imprisoned for refusing to take the Oath of Allegiance to take up his seat in Parliament, because they would not allow him to affirm.

"You cannot hope to build a better world without improving the individuals. To that end, each of us must work for our own improvement and, at the same time, share a general responsibility for all humanity, our particular duty being to aid those to whom we think we can be most useful."

MARIE CURIE (1867-1934)
WINNER OF THE NOBEL PRIZE FOR PHYSICS IN 1903 AND THE NOBEL PRIZE FOR CHEMISTRY IN 1911

## Ancient Greece and Rome

In Ancient Greece about 2,400 years ago, two philosophers called Leucippus and Democritus started talking of the world being made up of 'atoms' and the space around them – and nothing else.

Following on from these thinkers came Epicurus. His ideas were explained to Roman readers just over 2,000 years ago, when he wrote a long poem about what things are made of, and he said that nothing 'supernatural' exists.

## Europe

From 2,000 years ago to 1750, many people in Europe questioned whether there was a god or an afterlife, but most people were very cautious about it because they could be punished for saying such things. One of the first people to write a whole book saying that he believed that all we have is human life and no gods was Paul Heinrich Dietrich, who later became known as Baron D'Holbach. "The first concern of man is man," he said. A more inclusive way of putting it would be 'the first concern of humankind is the rest of humanity'. Let's remember that laws made by human beings are 'much more solid' than anything we might think come from gods, or 'divinities' as he called them.

From that time, millions of people have believed, talked about and written about believing that what we have is life, nature and atoms (including energy and sub-atomic activity!) – and just that.

33

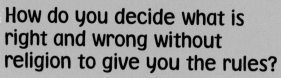

# Natalie Haynes

Natalie Haynes is a writer and broadcaster. She presents documentaries and reviews books, films, plays, television and art. Natalie was also a stand-up comedian for 12 years, before starting to write full time. We asked her about living a good life without gods and religion.

## How do you decide what is right and wrong without religion to give you the rules?

The simplest principle ('Would I like it if someone did that to me?') doesn't always work: what if you love spiders, and would like one as a birthday present? I hate spiders, and would loathe to be given one as a pet. So what might be right for you would be wrong for me.

But it works for a lot of things – would I like it if you took my things or hurt me? No. So I try to think about my choices that way.

Sometimes you can't help hurting people's feelings. But I always try not to, if I can.

Imagining yourself on the receiving end of your own behaviour is a good way to decide whether you're doing what you think is right or wrong…

## How can we work to make the world a better place without some sort of religious belief?

We can try to give more than we take. I know that sounds simple, but there it is. It doesn't matter if you can't make a difference on a global level. Most of us won't find the cure to a disease or discover clean

**66 Imagining yourself on the receiving end of your own behaviour is a good way to decide whether you're doing what you think is right or wrong… 99**

energy. But even on the smallest scale, you can make the people around you feel happier because you're there. It's hard sometimes, when you're in a bad mood, to be kind and thoughtful. But it pretty much always makes you feel better yourself if you make someone else happy. The secret about doing something nice for another person is this: it makes you feel good too.

## Do you have a strategy to help you live a good life?

Imagine a room filled with your friends and family and even people you know but aren't friends with – the bus driver, the newsagent, for example. You're in the room, but you have to leave early. Would they be sad that you'd gone? Would someone tell a story about how funny it was when you said or did something? Would someone else remember a time when you'd helped them out? Would people think of you as kind or unkind? I try to live as though this room exists, and I'd like my friends and family to be proud of how I behave, whether they are with me or not.

# How do humanists mark life's big events?

Humanists too like to mark the important events in life like birth, marriage and death – the rites of passage – in a special way. We do this without using religious rituals. Humanist organisations have developed ceremonies to help people acknowledge these occasions. The ceremonies are designed so that the people involved can create their own. The marriage ceremony has to include certain legal requirements, but apart from that, people are free to make the event as personal as they like, for example using words and music that are particularly significant for them and their friends and families.

You will see how Julia Adams and Jeff Round celebrated their wedding and their son's naming, and how Michael Rosen marked the death of his son.

JEFF AND JULIA
ON THEIR
WEDDING DAY

## Think about

Have you ever been to a secular birth, marriage or funeral ceremony?

How would you choose to mark these events?

## A day of celebration

Julia and Jeff had been together for five years before getting married, and they decided to have both their wedding and the naming ceremony for their son, Noel, at the same time. As humanists, they were able to design the whole day as they wanted it, with the help of a humanist celebrant. Here are extracts from the two ceremonies, which were conducted by Colin Swinburn, an accredited celebrant with the British Humanist Association.

# A wedding

JUST MARRIED!
HUMANIST CELEBRANT
COLIN SWINBURN
PRESENTS JULIA AND
JEFF WITH THEIR
MARRIAGE CERTIFICATE.

The celebrant started with these thoughts:

*"When two people openly and sincerely declare
their love for each other they are affirming the precious truth
that love is the foundation of all life.*

*For this couple, marriage involves a loving, giving and
honest relationship which includes fun and companionship.*

*It is based on equal freedom and identity of both
parties.*

*Marriage is a bond to be entered into only after
thought and reflection. As with life, it has its cycles,
its ups and downs – trials and triumphs.*

*It means sincere commitment to share each other's
joys and sorrows and to support and encourage each
other to grow and change in the years ahead."*

## Vows

CUTTING THE CAKE:
A TOWER OF
FAVOURITE BOOKS!

The celebrant asked Julia and Jeff if they came of their
own free will with the intention of continuing to be faithful
to each other in marriage. Then he asked them in turn if
they promised to share their lives as husband and wife, and
to make this commitment as a way of life for as long as they
both should live. They replied 'We do'.

Jeff and Julia said this to each other in turn:

*"I promise you that I will be your
husband/wife from this day forward,
to be faithful and honest in every way,
to honour the faith and trust you place in me,
to love and respect you in your successes and in your failures,
to make you laugh and to be there when you cry,
to care for you in sickness and in health,
and to be your companion and your friend,
on this journey that we make together."*

They then exchanged rings.

# A naming ceremony

**DURING THE CEREMONY**

The celebrant explained that throughout history, all over the world, ceremonies have been used to mark the important events in people's lives.

*"For humanists, the creation of the next generation is of unique importance. Our challenge is to leave behind a better world for future generations.*

*Julia and Jeff chose this non-religious humanist ceremony because they believe that their son should be free to make up his own mind about what he believes. That he should be able to explore the wonders of this world, discover for himself how the world works, learn respect and acceptance of others, and to lead an ethical and fulfilling life based on our common humanity."*

## Parents' commitment to Noel

Jeff and Julia made the following commitment to their son, Noel:

**SIGNING THE NAMING CERTIFICATE**

*"We will recognise your worth as a person, and help you to strengthen your sense of belonging to the human family. We will give you our love so that you may grow with trust in yourself and in other people. We will respect your right to be yourself and at the same time help you to understand the rights of others. We will encourage you always to search for the truth. We will give you the opportunity to develop your own understanding of life, and a respect for all living beings."*

## Formal naming

The celebrant then explained that the parents had brought Noel here to be welcomed by their family and friends, and to formally name him.

*"A name, once given, will be associated forever with a face, a voice, a walk, a laugh and all the other idiosyncrasies our family and friends recognise. The child's name will be spoken, whispered, shouted, cried, sung and written thousands of times impersonally or meaningfully by family, friends, neighbours, school fellows, teachers, doctors, colleagues, lovers, strangers, and maybe by children and grandchildren. It will define his identity."*

Julia and Jeff then gave Noel his full name: Noel Peter Huxley.

## Patentante and Patenonkel's commitment to Noel

The people concerned for a child's welfare include the immediate family and close relatives. In addition to the extended family, Julia and Jeff asked two people outside the family to make a commitment to give help and support at any future time should the need arise. In Germany, where Julia grew up, these roles are often referred to as Patentante and Patenonkel – 'Tante' means aunt and 'Onkel' uncle.

The celebrant asked Jeremy and Tanja if they agreed to offer friendship and sanctuary to Noel so that he could turn to them in times of doubt or difficulty with confidence and trust, and to give what support they could to Julia and Jeff as Noel's parents. Jeremy and Tanja agreed.

## Readings

Julia and Jeff chose two readings, one in German and the other from *Oh The Places You'll Go* by Dr Seuss. The ceremony also included a poem by Dorothy Law Nolte called *If Children Live with Tolerance*, which features the words:

A READING IN GERMAN

*"If children live with tolerance,*
*They learn to be patient…*
*If children live with love around them,*
*They learn to give love to the world."*

The celebrations ended with a concluding toast.

# A funeral

A humanist funeral is one where the people organising the funeral run it without mentioning a god or an 'afterlife'. For humanists, death is the last phase of life, and the purpose of a funeral is for the family and friends of the person who has died to remember them and celebrate their life. There are lots of ways of handling the death of someone. Here is one.

## MICHAEL ROSEN

"When my son Eddie died, it was a great shock and for a short while I thought it was unfair. Finding out about his illness, I discovered that it's just something that can happen to anyone.

Everyone who loved and knew Eddie wanted to talk about him. For over ten days, the house was full of people talking together, sometimes about Eddie, sometimes just being friendly. Very nearly everyone was very kind to me. That reminded me why I like being alive."

ONE OF THE PORTRAITS OF MICHAEL ROSEN BY QUENTIN BLAKE IN MICHAEL'S *SAD BOOK*. THE BOOK IS ANOTHER WAY OF REMEMBERING EDDIE.

## Eddie at home

"We also did something that some people found strange. We brought Eddie's body back into the house, so that people who wanted to could see him in his coffin. Some people did, some didn't. I looked at him many times. It's how I learned that he really was dead; he hadn't gone away, or disappeared. His body had stopped working. And I could see that it had. Sometimes I stroked his head. That's part of how I know and love Eddie."

## The funeral

"Then we had a funeral where we played some of Eddie's favourite music, people who loved him stood up and told stories about him, read poems they had written for him. His brother Joe and a group of young people carried his coffin. He was cremated. The woman who ran the ceremony was Eddie's old head teacher. As it happens, she's a religious person, but as a humanist I was able to recognise and appreciate that she would run the ceremony really well, and in a secular way, for all of us in the room with our different beliefs, faiths and no faith.

Different members of the family have done different things with his ashes. His step-sister threw some over a cliff in Cornwall when there was an eclipse. Others poured some into the ground underneath a stone in a cemetery. The stone has the dates of Eddie's life and a little quotation from a poem my father wrote for him: *Larger than life.*"

## Remembering Eddie

"We've done many different things to remember Eddie: his old school had a poetry competition named after him; the hockey team he used to play for had a shield named after him, for the best young player each year; every year on the anniversary of when he died, the whole family get together and have a big meal."

# Shappi Khorsandi

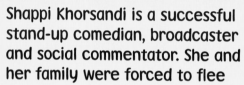

Shappi Khorsandi is a successful stand-up comedian, broadcaster and social commentator. She and her family were forced to flee from Iran when she was a child, after her father published a satirical poem against the new regime. We asked her about how her upbringing has informed her personal philosophy.

## My mum and dad never took us to religious places, or prayed, or told us there was a god.

At school some teachers believed in god and talked to us about it. We sang hymns in assembly. I really liked singing hymns. I still do. I really like singing with a whole lot of people, it makes me feel uplifted, but the songs don't have to be religious.

## Do we need religious books to tell us what is right and what is wrong?

I know the Bible and other religious books are full of stories to help people know right from wrong. I know some of the stories. But I can understand right from wrong without these books. I can question myself and try and be honest about why I behave in certain ways. For example, I have learned that there is no such thing as helping someone and not getting anything in return because helping someone makes you feel good inside. That's what you get and that is enough.

## I have also learned to treat other people the way I would like to be treated, with respect and kindness.

When I was younger, I was mean to people sometimes. Sometimes, when I was jealous of someone I did mean things like ignore them or say rude things about them to other people. I learned that doing this made me feel bad inside. So I stopped doing it and it made a big difference to my life. My life got happier. More people wanted to be my friend, more people trusted me and helped me when I needed help.

> **I believe we can be kind just because we are human.**

## My parents taught me to share.

It was very important to my parents to teach me to be polite and caring. They taught me to say 'please' and 'thank you'. They taught me to not just share, but to give things away when another kid wanted it, or needed it more than me. Like the last sweet or a book, or a really huge stick I'd found.

I still forget to be kind and generous sometimes because I get wrapped up in what I want. My dad is very good at reminding me to put my feet in other people's shoes when I get like this. When I do that, I see what I wanted wasn't worth all the fuss, although this can take a while.

## Why should we be kind?

I believe we can be kind just because we are human. Being kind is doing something for someone without being asked, or noticing how they are feeling without being told. Being kind is helping someone else and not wanting anything in return, even if it makes you late for work or school, or costs you some money or makes you tired. It makes you connected with a positive energy, it feels like you helped turn the world a little.

# What next?

The main idea of this book is getting you to think about humanism and religion. You could also say that it's a book about values – that is, what different people believe about what is good or right, especially when it comes to how best to live their lives. One way to get thinking about these things is to start with the questions we've asked throughout the book.

This is a book that you don't have to read by starting at the beginning and then reading one page after another. You can skim through it, looking for questions that start you thinking. Or you can look for headings and titles that interest you. Perhaps some things in the book will make you stop and think, or you'll see something you strongly disagree with. That's a good reason for reading a bit more on that page too!

If you're reading this book in school, there may be things in it that you would like to talk about with your parents or whoever looks after you, or with someone else you trust. You might find it useful to copy out that part so that you're sure you've understood what it says.

And it's worth remembering that it's perfectly OK:

- to change your mind about things
- to be not sure about things
- to go on changing your mind and being not
  sure for the whole of your life.

# What do you think?

Now that you've read the book, what things do you think religious and non-religious people agree on? Where do you think you find humanists?

Here are are the questions we've asked:

## What's most important

What are the things that are important to you?
Do you think you should behave as if you have only one life?

# God and religion

Do you believe in a god?
If yes, what does that belief mean to you?
If you don't believe in a god, why not?

# Tolerance

Do you think we should be tolerant of other people's beliefs?
If you do, why is it important?
If you don't, why not?
Either way, how does this affect how you behave?

# Morality

Do you think there is an afterlife, or a day of judgement after you die, when it's decided whether you go to heaven or hell?
If you do, how does that affect the way you behave?
If not, how does that affect your behaviour?

What do you think about the Golden Rule?
Would the world be a better place if everyone acted in this way?

How do you decide for yourself whether to lie or not – especially if no one else is going to find out?

# The purpose of life

What do you think is the purpose of life?

# The statement of values

What do you think about these values?
Which values are most important for you?

# The origins of life

What do you think about the origins of life and what the scientists say?
How does that compare with what the major religions say?
What do you think?

# Celebrations and ceremonies

Have you ever been to a secular birth, marriage or funeral ceremony?
How would you choose to mark these events?
How would you like to be remembered when you die?

## Festivals

Most humanists are happy to take part in the traditional rituals of family gatherings and present giving at Christmas, without any religious observances, and in the giving of Easter eggs and chocolate at Easter. Are there any other festivals you know about, from other cultures or traditions? Can you think of any other occasions which you would like to mark in some way with a festival?

## Your personal charter for living a good life

Now that you have thought about all these questions, try to write a 'charter' for yourself: a set of values for how to live your life. Use these headings from the Statement of Values to help you. We've given you an example of how you could begin each of them, but of course you can use your own words. You can also add some headings of your own.

### The self
I value myself as a human being capable of moral, intellectual and spiritual development, and I will strive for knowledge, wisdom and understanding. I will…

### Relationships
I value others for themselves and I will respect and care for others…

### Society
I value truth, justice, human rights and freedom. I will be a responsible citizen and…

### The environment
I value the environment, both natural and shaped by humanity, as the basis of life. I accept my responsibility to future generations, and will…

# Glossary

**affirm** make a formal declaration in court rather than taking an oath

**altruism** a selfless and disinterested (unbiased) concern for the well-being of others

**empathy** the ability to understand and share the feelings of another

**ethics/ethical** moral principles that govern a person's behaviour or the conducting of an activity

**evolution** the process by which different kinds of living organism are believed to have developed from earlier forms during the history of the Earth

**fossils** the remains or impression of a prehistoric plant or animal embedded in rock and preserved in petrified form

**morals/morality/moral values** concerned with the principles of right and wrong behaviour

**philosophy/philosophies** the study of the fundamental nature of knowledge, reality and existence

# Useful information

Here are some websites and books you might find interesting:

**British Humanist Association** https://humanism.org.uk

**American Humanist Association** http://americanhumanist.org

**Council of Australian Humanist Societies** http://humanist.org.au

## Humanism and schools

If you go to a state school, your parents have the right to withdraw you from Religious Studies and any act of worship. Most humanists think that it's a good idea to study religion in schools but think that there should be no worship in schools.

**Humanism Canada** http://www.humanistcanada.ca

**Kids Company** http://www.kidsco.org.uk

*The Young Atheist's Handbook: Lessons for Living a Good Life Without God* by Alom Shaha, Biteback Publishing

*Big Bang* by Heather Couper and Nigel Henbest, published by Dorling Kindersley. And *Is Anybody Out There?* by the same authors

*From the Beginning* by Katie Edwards and Brian Rosen, published by the Natural History Museum

*Time and the Universe* by Mary and John Gribbin, published by Hodder

*Evolve or Die* by Phil Gates, Hippo Horrible Science series

And, for a list of recommended books on evolution and the beginnings of the world and life, see:

**https://humanism.org.uk/ education/recommended-resources/**

# Index